Flowers Coloring Book
Beautiful Garden Flowers Coloring Book For Adult

Adriana P. Jenova

Published by PUBLISHING COMPANY in 2015
First edition: First printing
Illustrations and design © 2015 Adriana P. Jenova

Author Contact
allcoloringbook.com

ISBN-13: 978-1522789291
ISBN-10: 1522789294

www.ingramcontent.com/pod-product-compliance
Lightning Source LLC
Chambersburg PA
CBHW081158280526
45787CB00008B/3378